FAIR HELEN

Poems to My Wife

Gene Edwards

TABLE OF CONTENTS

DEDICATION

To
My Two Daughters
The beauty of their mother
reigns perfect in her two daughters,
Lynda and Cindy.

FROM WHENCE CAME THE TITLE OF THESE POEMS?

Some nine hundred years before Christ, there lived in Greece a blind poet named Homer. He told many fanciful stories that are still loved and read today. Blind Homer wrote an ageless story of Paris of Troy. On a visit to Greece, Paris, as the story was told, fell in love with a Greek girl with the beauty of a goddess. Their love launched the Trojan Wars.

In writing the story, Homer placed these words in the mouth of Paris of Troy upon first seeing the face of Helen:

"Fair Helen, make me immortal with a kiss."

That feeling was not too far from mine when first I ever saw the face of another Helen.

THE FIRST TIME EVER I SAW YOUR FACE

There are things to be found in church
Beyond ritual, word and penitence,
Things of danger against which
A young, unwary man has no defense.

For there was a summer morn when
Among the worshippers I took my usual place
And idly watched stained glass
Windows light and color lace

And just as idly glanced up
To pulpit and then to choir,
There to see a face
Only heaven's vaults could inspire.

Then stood this living work of art
And to us began to sing,
While light from resplendent windows
Enrobed this delicate thing.

(continued)

And marked I the place where
Was fettered my willing heart
To this celebration of beauty,
Crafted by angelic art.

Soon the meeting ended,
We rose, and someone prayed.
The crowd departed, save for this poor soul,
Who, immovable, quietly stayed.

For etched upon my sight was
A scene I would forever bear:
'Twas a girl so soft,
So delicate, so fair.

Then looking up, I this living vision saw
As she came passing by,
A train of loveliness who filled my heart
Even as she stole my eye.

Her face, her form,
Her grace, her charm
So pleased my eye,
I knew that I would love her until I die.

THE EVENING I MET YOU

Someone asked, "Have you met Helen?"
"Yes," sang my heart, "or so it seems."
For I had traced that face
Within a thousand dreams.

There beside the church,
Beneath a budding tree,
Fate made so evident
Its scheme for me.

For before me in miniature stood
All beauty nature can bestow.
You smiled, and by such a chain
Made a captive of my soul.

You spoke, and by that weapon
Martyred this fainting heart.
Naught now but your slave,
Yet I had gained the better part.

(continued)

So was born my bondage:
Ne'er again would I be free.
Yet never in all the passing years
Have I ever asked for liberty.

It was an enchanted moment
Within an enchanted day,
Nor has its memory ever
From me slipped away.

No king with all his riches
Has ever owned so much,
For on that hallowed evening
I had fair Helen touched.

THE PLOT

My eye, my ear,

My wit, my heart

Did see, did hear

And then did love

Your face, your voice, your style,

As living art.

You charmed, you pleased,

Confounded, delighted,

And brashly walked

Into my heart.

Then did my skill, my soul,

My body and my thought

Draw, entice,

Persuade and devise

A way to keep you there

Forever as my prize.

Because you were kind, true,

Comely and passion-wise,

So did I work, contrive,

And cast off fear

To make you my love, my light,

(continued)

5

My life, my dear.
Earth, hell, sanity, flame and folly
I defied
To keep you near, in my heart,
By my side.
So now, my heart, my wit,
My will, my ear, my eye
Make daily plans to keep, to hold
And to love you
Until I die.

MOST BEAUTIFUL OF ALL

What are the most beautiful things

The eye can sight?

A gliding swan all robed in white,

A bounding deer in startled flight,

A dancing horse at prancing play,

A woman of beauty in full array.

Of these, which is the most beautiful of all?

Which does most the heart and mind enthrall?

Search out every valley, every mountain,

Poll the stars, inquire of heaven.

The answers are but one,

`Tis thee, my beloved Helen.

EDEN'S SECOND DAUGHTER

Eden's second daughter this:

All that is beauty, all that is bliss.

Thy tressed locks of stardust strewn,

Thy body of living ivory hewn.

In thee perfect grace and perfect charm

Perfect blend.

The face of God

Thy face is kin.

Thou art that space where dims the line

Of things of earth and things divine.

The Night It Snowed

I stepped upon the stage and with keen eyes looked about, for it was my first time there since I had learned it was, indeed, a stage, and I a player on it.

For a long time I simply stood there on the rough pine flooring and watched the other players as they contemplated their assigned roles, their script, the lines which had been given them to speak.

My part was almost always but a nameless figure lost somewhere in the passing crowd. As time went on, I noted each player was at last allowed to come center stage, there to speak his most telling lines, pause, and pass back again into the faceless crowd. I watched and wondered just what my lines might one day be.

In most of my scenes I was but an actor whiling away my day, speaking with friends and passersby. But on one such dull occasion there came upon the set, entering stage left, a girl of such beauty as I had never seen. Captivated, yet far too shy to speak, another in merciful pity brought me to her and introduced me to this convocation of charm, this celebration of beauty.

The scenes changed. Time passed. Scenes changed again, and yet again. Each time I spied this lovely creature on the set, I found some reason to speak to her some part of the script which was given me to say. Always she let me know that we would not play leading roles together, for her future roles would be played out in far distant places or wherever else the Producer might choose for her to speak her lines.

And though I continued to find myself near her, and mumbled to her some senseless, inane thought I found in my script, she never let me near enough to touch her, much less to do what my heart longed to do: to take her in my arms, kiss her, and so capture her heart that we might play out all our roles and scenes together. Alas, it was painfully evident this dream would never be my lot.

Then, one day suddenly and unexpectedly, or so I thought, it began to snow. It was the longest, deepest snow the stage had seen within any of our lifetimes. And it was in that very moment I realized I was alone upon the stage with that child of Venus, that daughter of Helen of Troy.

(continued)

I looked quickly about the stage. The other players had simply vanished. And it was night. The set was captivating. We were seated together, alone in an old car, on a deserted, snow-covered road. All was as still as it was enchanted. Boldly, but in terror, I slipped my arm about her shoulder, hardly allowing it to even touch her. To my everlasting astonishment, she reached up, touched my hand and gently placed my arm around her.

Time stopped. I looked about the stage again, this time to discover that somehow I now stood at center stage, a place I had never been. *This* was my hour. I turned again and gazed upon that lovely face, glowing like angelic light. Then to her I spoke these words: Shakespeare said that life is a stage and we the players on it. If this be so, then here is my most important line:

Oh, Helen, you know I love you.

Her reply was beyond all the hope for which my heart might dare to wish, for she replied: "Oh, Gene, I love you with all my heart."

(continued)

At that, I took this living enchantment into my arms and kissed her, even as she kissed me. In so doing, I knew beyond all doubt that if I shared this stage with a million other souls, this hallowed night had been marked off for us alone.

The scene ended. We exited stage right. The set grew dim. The curtain closed. I did not know if I would ever again play opposite this girl, nor for that matter, if I did, what our roles might be.

I was content to know that I had been given one of the choicest of all roles, for I had been cast with this grecian goddess, the very essence of all that is feminine beauty, in a role that was, of all things, an incomparably beautiful, breathtaking *love scene.*

The name of the play came to be known as:
The Night it Snowed.

OUR WEDDING DAY

I have, this memorable day,
Won that girl who is
Beauty at its farthest reach,
A walking, living spectrum
Of the feminine mystique.
In her all ideals of womanhood
Become a living shrine.
In her face night stars and day sun
In mystery combine;
But from her countenance
Both at once do shine.
Where then her reigning throne
And where her sceptered seat,
That you incarnate beauty
May gaze upon and greet?
From this day on, only in
My heart or in my arms
Shall you this goddess meet.

THE VOW
(The morning after our wedding)

I awoke this morning to view

Things I never dreamt nor ever knew:

My Bible on the table, your clothes upon the floor—

Incongruous to one who never oneness knew before.

Lithe arms, and hands as warm as fire,

Your fashion the kindling of desire,

A face you surely from heaven stole.

These graces gather into one living whole

And swarm my senses, drown my unbelieving eyes,

As this thought captures, then enraptures my soul:

That guiltless I have loved this one who beside me lies.

Then comes this mystery into view:

That graces given but to swans and you,

Such splendor to me has been sent

For whatever days or years with you have to me been lent.

Men, `tis said, give love but the corner of their lives;

All else is spent for some temporal prize.

Love is but the gladiator's rest,

His draught before the battle and the quest.

I gaze at you who lie so closely to my side

And know that another chart shall be my guide.

Awake, my love, our journey has begun.

My life and loving you shall ever be but one.

I SPOKE TO A ROSE

Today I spoke to a rose,

One as shy, yet as lovely as thee.

Go, flower of beauty, so tender and so young,

Speak to my love who, as you,

In beauty does abide,

But who desires not to be known

Nor even spied.

Tell her, had you in some lonely desert sprung,

There to live, to die, with none your

Loveliness to share,

Nor word of such splendor ever to others bare,

No gain for any there would be

Of beauty so hidden, so retired.

Ask my love to with you join

And suffer herself to be admired,

To be seen, to be watched, and to be desired.

Having spoken so, dear rose, then die,

That my love may see how quickly passes by

The brief moments bequeathed to those of beauty rare.

What little time have they their loveliness to share.

(continued)

Perhaps my love will then come forth to display,

Not once to one, but to all each day,

Beauty's rarest gifts, so exotic and so fair.

LOVE'S CHAINED NOT
(Written while traveling on a train crossing
Switzerland and on to Prague)

Today as I took my place upon this train

That would carry me through rugged Alps' terrain,

There spoke from vaults within my heart

That ne'er had we been so far apart:

Not since that summer's day

My heart did find and love thee.

As I looked down from mountains high and grand,

I saw distant valley lands.

Later on, as we crossed the lowest plains,

I looked up to see the mountains brush the sky.

Yet, all the while the sun, in its long run,

With single eye watched over you and watched over me.

Then, as the sun finished its run,

There came to us, in place of brightest light,

That lovely lady night.

She, from deepest, darkest skies,

Found us with her ten thousand eyes.

(continued)

21

Be thou in valleys or on the mountain highs,

Be thou on earth or in those distant skies,

Love's chained not by miles,

Nor nights, nor days.

As sun and stars above thee,

My heart this day found and loved thee.

DISTRACTED

We have a question we'd like to ask you:

You had breakfast with President Kennedy
and Billy Graham.

How did the morning fare?

How could I possibly know—

Helen was not there.

A banquet was given in your honor. People
came from far and near.

How did the evening go?

Helen sat beside me—

How could I possibly know?

THE EPITAPH

If I should go before thee

To realms which are eternal;

Or should you shed the outer cloak

And be the first to be immortal;

It matters not.

Though storms of light do thee enfold,

Or God himself be thine abode,

Yet shall I find that holy place,

And there, far better shall I love thee.

GeneEdwards888@gmail.com
www.GeneEdwards.com